GREEN EMBRACES
IDENTITY RECLAIMED

"You were Meant for More" Series

TAMARA J. BUCHAN
LINDSEY D. OSBORNE

RECLAIM
MINISTRIES

SANTA ROSA
CALIFORNIA

ISBN-13: 978-1506166957
ISBN-10: 1506166954

Quoted Scripture:
Scripture quotations marked NRSV are taken from the New Revised Standard Version Bible, copyright 1989, Division of Christian Education of the National Council of the Churches of Christ in the United States of America. Used by permission. All rights reserved.
Quoted Scripture from BibleGateway.com:

Scripture quotations marked NIV are taken from the HOLY BIBLE, NEW INTERNATIONAL VERSION®. NIV®. Copyright © 1973, 1978, 1984, 2011 by Biblica, Inc.™ Used by permission. All rights reserved worldwide.

Scripture quotations marked NLT are taken from the Holy Bible. New Living Translation copyright© 1996, 2004, 2007 by Tyndale House Foundation. Used by permission of Tyndale House Publishers, Inc. Carol Stream, Illinois 60188. All rights reserved.

Scripture quotations marked NASB are taken from the New American Standard Bible, © 1960, 1962, 1963, 1968, 1971, 1972, 1973, 1975, 1977, 1995 by The Lockman Foundation. Used by permission.

Scripture quotations marked KJ21 are taken from the 21st Century King James Version®, Copyright © 1994. Used by permission of Deuel Enterprises, Inc., Gary, SD 57237. All rights reserved.

Scripture quotations marked NKJV are taken from the New King James Version®. Copyright © 1982 by Thomas Nelson, Inc. Used by permission. All rights reserved.

Scripture quotations marked KJV are taken from the Holy Bible, King James Version which is in the public domain.Scripture quotations marked ASV are taken from the American Standard Version Bible, which is in the public domain.

Cover Art and Design: Andrew and Brenda Emmert.
Publishing Manager/Graphic Design: Anne Thompson, www.ebookannie.com.

For all who are led by the Spirit of God are children of God. For you did not receive a spirit of slavery to fall back into fear, but you have received a spirit of adoption. When we cry, "Abba! Father!" it is that very Spirit bearing witness with our spirit that we are children of God, and if children, then heirs, heirs of God and joint heirs with Christ.

Romans 8:14-17

You were Meant for More

A strong handshake, a tender hug, a long embrace...being held feels good. As human beings built for connection, embraces carry power when they come from someone who knows us fully and loves us anyways.

The embrace of God's powerfully loving arms began in a green garden long ago. The original design was a clean, lively, and green creation to host and hold people as they were meant to be. To lived loved was the original design. We've wandered and gotten lost, lived for less, and walked a winding road. However, the fresh, pure, living embrace of God who knows us as Beloved Child, is available to each of us, right now. It's up to us to reclaim what was ours all along.

Dedication

Green Embraces: Identity Reclaimed is dedicated to you,
as one of God's beloved children who may not know
the depth to which your Heavenly Father, adores you.
He speaks his word of affirmation over you,
just like he did for his first son, Jesus:
"You are my beloved child,
in whom I take great delight."

Foreword

In John 8:36, Jesus says, "If the Son sets you free, you will be free indeed." We all long for freedom and yet so often the pain and guilt and shame of our past imprisons us and gets in the way of truly experiencing the kind of freedom and the kind of abundant, joyful life that Jesus offers to each one of us.

I have worked with teenagers through the ministry of Young Life for the past thirty-five years. I can honestly say that the number one issue facing young people is this lack of identity, a lack of knowing who they truly are as individuals created in the image of God with the capacity to know Him personally. To watch young people discover the truth of their identity, is to see them set free and to see them discover, for the first time, their God-given purpose and destiny. And it isn't just young people. People of all ages in our world today are struggling to find peace and so often **the root issue** is simply this - not knowing who they truly are and whose they are.

In this book, ***Green Embraces: Identity Reclaimed***, Tamara J. Buchan and Lindsey D. Osborne have offered a concise, succinct, powerful window into what it means for us to deny the lies of our past and to embrace the truth of who we really are in Christ. The words presented here, help us to discover that we are truly loved, that our story is part of a greater divine story, that we are forgiven and truly accepted and that we have a true place of belonging. If embraced, these words have the power to bring true freedom, the kind of freedom that can only come when we see ourselves the way that God sees us, a beloved child of the King!

Pam Moore, *Director of Training*
Young Life

Preface

When Jesus walked the earth, he knew he wanted to communicate to people in the regular, everyday parts of their life. They'd heard the religious leaders speak for years, but it often felt so far away from what they did on a daily basis. They longed to know someone understood them, and cared about the desires they carried deep within their hearts.

Jesus found ways to relate to the people through both words and experiences.

He taught them and then he followed his teachings up with experiences which equipped the people to both hear it, see it, and often touch and taste it. In the process, people were transformed and their lives were never the same.

Here's a practical example. Early in his ministry, Jesus asked Peter the fisherman to use his boat to teach the crowds which were practically pushing him into the lake in their eagerness to hear (Luke 5:1-11). After Jesus finished, he asked Peter to go out to the middle of the lake and to put down his nets. Peter, being the experienced fisherman, knew that at noon on a hot day no fish would be caught near the surface of the water....they would be deep down at the bottom of the lake. But, not wanting to disrespect his new friend Jesus, he replied, "I've worked all night and didn't catch anything, *but because you say so*, I will let the nets down again."

He put down the nets and the boat became so full of fish, it began to sink.

At that moment, Peter knew that everything Jesus said was true because he experienced in living color. He fell to his knees and worshipped Jesus. After his worship, he gave his whole life to following Jesus.

Jesus began his ministry with Peter's haul of fish and he ended his ministry with Peter and another haul of fish. This time it was early morning after his resurrection and he stood on the beach calling out, "Friends, have you caught any fish?"

Having fished all night without success, they discouragingly replied, "No, not one."

Jesus instructed, ***"Throw your nets on the other side of the boat*** and you will get some."

They did and once again, the haul of fish was so great, they barely got the boat to shore!

I am following Jesus' instruction to throw my nets to the other side of the boat because he wants to see a big haul of fish—people who truly know him, not information about him they've been taught in church or private Christian school, or seen on the internet, but in a living, breathing relationship where we live life together.

Because after all, we were created for relationship.

This is my purpose in creating this book.

I want to speak the language of the culture through technology, links, video, small liberties with Scripture, (which keep the intent but make it more applicable) and experiences which take information and transform it into truth!

So then, let's do life together with the God who created us and loves us and wants our very best in lives. For He knows "You were Meant for More!"

TABLE OF CONTENTS

Before reading Chapter 1, watch the video: *My Invitation from the Lord*. Go to, http://vimeo.com/95551691 or scan the QR Code (If unable to view, read script at the end of the book).

CHAPTER *1*

AN OFFICIAL CHANGE

The formation of who you are, of your identity, flows
from your family. No matter how broken, absent, bat-
tered, bruised or blessed your family may be, they are
from whom you came. You were born you because of the people
who came before you.

But maybe, who we are and where we come from, is borne
not from the collision between sperm and egg, but rather from
a different family altogether. Perhaps your story is adoption.
Biology alone does not determine our identity or our family.
Adoption is a powerful, transformative and ancient process.
Adoption happens in the earthly realm, yes, and always has.
But adoption also begins for all of us, in a kingdom, with a
Parent who has a heart yearning for us and unconditional love
ready to envelop us.

Consider these two questions from God:

Do you know how much I love you?

15

Do you know what it means to be adopted into my family?

I was stunned when I read Romans 8:14-17 that day, as I discovered I had two very important identities: one as an adopted child, and one as a royal heir:

> For all who are led by the Spirit of God are children of God. For you did not receive a spirit of slavery to fall back into fear, but you have received a spirit of adoption. When we cry, "Abba! Father!" it is that very Spirit bearing witness with our spirit that we are children of God, if children, then heirs, heirs of God and joint heirs with Christ—if, in fact, we suffer with him so that we may also be glorified with him.

Compared to today, adoptions were very different when the Apostle Paul wrote his letter to the Church of Rome. At times when an heir was needed, even adults were sometimes adopted into a Roman family. The family and the heir went before the judge, who had a parchment that included all the facts about the future heir's life.

The judge would announce the adoption, and then declare that all that had come before that moment was completely erased. And, with some drama, he would take the rag and wipe the parchment clean, in order for the adoptee to write his or her new name.

Not only was the adopted heir given a fresh start, seven mentors would come forward to sign their name as ones who would teach them how to live their new life.

Take a moment to envision your own adoption into the family of God.

Imagine you are leaving the brokenness or loneliness of the family you have known. Even if you have an endearing earthly family, the invitation to God's greater family, as the ultimate reality, awaits you.

If you are standing in the courtroom, waiting for the official adoption, what is on your list of life facts? What has defined your story? Think of your list of accomplishments, occupations, education, experiences, wins and losses. Is there anything you would want washed off of your parchment paper history?

What are you feeling with God, the Father, in the room just across the way? Is it fear? Anticipation? Excitement? Embarrassment? Neutrality? Exhausted? Any and all emotions are welcome in this moment.

What are your past ideas or issues with God that need to be aired in this negotiating stage? What questions will you ask? What stories will God tell?

God does not adopt us alone. Rather, we are entering into a huge community. Who else is in the family room? Who else do you know who is being adopted today? And who else has been adopted before you that you will see around the banquet table?

Finally, who are the seven mentors who will gather around you, excitedly and intentionally standing alongside to welcome you into this new family?

Who are seven people who might sign up to help you in your formation and transformation as God's new kid?

How often do you read Luke 3? Its second half of it is the genealogy of Jesus. Pretty dull stuff, right? Well, one day, I read it, because the Lord had directed me to it. I was surprised to see the very last line: "Adam was the son of God." Hmmm, that surprised me. I knew that God created Adam, but I never thought of him as the "son of God."

I began to consider the difference it made that Adam and Eve were created as "children of God" rather than just the "first people." I began to understand my Heavenly Father in a different way: **he created all of us, so that we could be his kids.**

His kids. I liked the sound of that.

My imagination began to flow to big family dinners around a massive round table, one where everyone was present.

The food was delicious, and the laughter spontaneous.

I envisioned birthdays where each child was honored, and gifts were given in abundance.

I smiled when I thought of other children brought into the family and the big welcome they were given!

Reflect

1. *Look back:* What memories of growing up in family do you have? Are they mostly happy? Sad? Painful? Chaotic? Peaceful? Boring? Split between a "before" and "after" event? Growing up, what was different about friends' families from your own?

2. *Take inventory:* What are the blessings of being a child? What are the struggles and frustrations kids feel?

3. *Dream forward:* Do you have a family now? Do you want one? As a parent, what ideals, principals, values, and descriptions do you want to have in your own family?

DO something!

1. Learn the origin of your name. Why were you given your name? Does it mean anything to you? If you have named a child or a pet, think back to how you came to choose that name. Does that name say anything about who they are?

2. Think about someone you know by a nickname. **Have a conversation with friends this week, about how what we are called impacts how we are known.** Does our identity stem from our name? Or does it stem from the people who gave it to us?

Before reading Chapter 2, watch the video: *Orphan Story*. Go to, https://vimeo.com/97771271 or scan the QR Code (If unable to view, read script at the end of the book).

RAGS, BAGS AND DADS

C an you relate to the little girl sleeping with her bag of rags on concrete?

1. What does the beginning of your story hold? What rags are in your bags? What were the major experiences that shaped your childhood? What did you package away from those experiences that you have carried through life with you?

2. Can you follow your bag of rags through different times of your life? When have you passed up on something new and freeing because you were still tied up with the bag of rags?

I had not fully embraced my adoption in his Father's family. I often continued to live like the orphan I was before my salvation.

The day my Heavenly Father revealed to me that I was like her was a big wake-up call.

I was safe and secure in my salvation through my belief in Jesus and in forgiveness through his sacrifice on the cross.

And yet, I realized, to simply live saved was not enough.

I have discovered the difference between being saved and being adopted.

God desires so much more for us than our salvation from sin.

God has abundant life available for us.

Salvation is not simply a removal of sin or a change in behavior.

Instead, salvation is an invitation to complete reconciliation.

We have the opportunity to return to how we were created to live.

We have the chance to live a just and whole relationship with God, fully accepted, absolutely loved, invited to live a true and abundant life.

When we realize Jesus came to earth to show us how to live as kids in his father's family, we begin to discover a whole new life awaits us, one we have never known before.

We have been invited into a family that functions in a healthy way. We have parents who want to spend time hearing about our day at the dinner table.

We have a family that gathers to spend time together in the Great Room, a place where fun, laughter and friendly competition takes place.

We have a beautiful bedroom where we enjoy rest, deep sleep, and a chance to be alone to reflect and to imagine all the opportunities that lie ahead.

We also have new clothes, ones that replace the old bag of

rags we keep wearing and toting around.

Our new clothes are designed just for us; they are the clothes of Jesus' righteousness, which cleanse us and set us free.

His clothes on us make us beautiful and secure, identifying us as part of his family.

We are God's treasure. We are God's beloved, cherished, celebrated and secure child.

Reflect:

1. *Look back:* Who gave you the ragged clothes you still keep? What experiences in life "shredded your hopes and dreams?"

2. *Take inventory:* What rags do you really hold on to, even today?

3. *Dream forward:* What would it mean to throw away the bag of rags? Could you do it? Would you?

Do Something:

This week as you hold a rag, washing your body in the shower, sponging off your car, or wiping down a countertop, think about what you carry. Remember the story of the adopted orphan girl and the reflection questions you answered. Begin to let go of a ragged experience, naming it as you wring out your rags this week.

CHAPTER 3

BACK TO THE BEGINNING OF THE STORY

Do you remember my discovery that Adam and Eve were created to be God's kids? I always like to go back to the beginning of a story. Let's check in with Adam and Eve to see how life in the Garden of Eden suits them.

The word "*eden*" means a delightful place, paradise; a state of great delight, happiness or contentment, bliss (freedictionary.com).

Our Creator had a vision for our lives: to be in relationship with him, and to live as royalty in the Garden.

Genesis 1:26-28 (NLT) states:

Then God said, "Let us make human beings in our image, to be like us. They will reign over the fish in the sea, the birds in the sky, the livestock, all the wild animals on the earth, and the small animals that scurry along the ground."

So, God created human beings in his own image. In the image of God, he created them; male and female, he created them.

Then God blessed them and said, "Be fruitful and multiply. Fill the earth and govern it. Reign over the fish in the sea, the birds in the sky, and all the animals that scurry along the ground.

Imagine it.

Adam and Eve were to be like their Creator Parents. They were to govern and reign over all creation.

They had the ability to be creative, to be productive, and to partner together with each other and with God to create a garden of "*eden*": a place of great delight, paradise, bliss and happiness.

One of the coolest parts about the garden was the reality of God's presence within it. We know he walked in the garden and he spoke to them (Genesis 3:8).

Have you ever wondered if God sees you? Or knows you? Or loves you?

Adam and Eve never had to wonder.

They had it all.

That is, until they listened to a wily serpent over their father, giving in to temptation instead of continuing to trust.

It was in the moment of choosing to eat from the one tree they had been told to stay away from, the Tree of the Knowledge of Good and Evil, that everything changed.

Completely.

Forever.

In one quick decision, Adam and Eve stopped trusting the heart of their father for them and began to believe the lie of the serpent that:

He couldn't be trusted

     He was withholding from them

He didn't have their best at heart

In essence, Adam and Eve rejected God as their parent the very moment they turned away from his protection and provision, transgressing the one limit he had lovingly set before them.

The orphan identity has been around from the beginning of time. Its purpose is to convince us, like the first children, to mistrust our father's motives, heart, and plans for us. No wonder God cried out, "What have you done?" Life has never been the same.

Reflect:

1. *Look back:* What are your earliest memories of what you believed about God?

2. *Take inventory:* How comfortable are you in depending on others? Are you able to trust that provision will come without you working on it yourself? Is it easy or challenging for you to allow other people to help you? Can you wait for something to come that has been promised?

3. *Dream forward:* Imagine a right relationship with God. What would make you feel ultimately relieved in a dependent relationship with the Parent who loves to lovingly and completely provide?

Do Something:

Depend on someone else this week. If you're heading somewhere you usually travel to alone, invent a carpool opportunity and let them give the ride. If you usually refuse offers of help, listen closely for one this week and accept it. Pay attention to the emotions, thoughts, and feelings you have when someone else is freely and deliberately helping you.

CHAPTER 4

GOD'S VISION FOR US IN RELATIONSHIPS

We were created by God for two reasons:
to live in relationship with him,
and to partner with him in meaningful work.

Have you ever woken up feeling utterly and totally alone? Are you ever overwhelmed by the responsibility of providing for yourself or family, or the pressures and treadmill pace of work that never seems finished? It's easy to feel overwhelmed by loneliness and responsibility. The good news, however, is that when we discover the depth of our Heavenly Father's desire for us, it changes everything!

God wasn't content to exist in heaven with just one son. Instead, he wanted a great big family where everyone matters!

God wanted so many children that when He went into the Garden, he had children everywhere, each with their own unique personality and gifts which would contribute to creating heaven on earth.

You are one that he dreamed about at creation.

You are one with whom he longs to share life.

You are one upon whom he has gifted with unique talents and gifts, which contribute to building his kingdom on earth.

God's connection with human beings is deliberate, unique, and life-changing. Ephesians 1:3 tells us, ". . .the Father of our Lord Jesus Christ has blessed us **with every spiritual blessing in the heavenly realms. . . "**

So, what blessings do we find in heaven?

- Life

- Peace

- Joy

- Love

- Unbroken connection with God

- Beauty

- Healthy bodies

- Completeness

- Synergy

- Unconditional acceptance

- Belonging

What's not in heaven?

- Depression

- Disease
- Fear
- Fighting
- Rejection
- Abuse
- War
- Poverty
- Failure
- Abandonment
- Shame

Sometimes I think heaven feels ethereal, so I like to think about the Garden of Eden and what it was like. After all, God created Eden to be heaven on earth. Adam and Eve would have lived forever if they continued to eat the fruit from the Tree of Life.

So, what was in the Garden of Eden?

Full access to God—He walked amongst his kids, sharing their joy in the growth of the garden, celebrating all the different animals.

Complete oneness between Adam and Eve—Can you imagine what it would be like to have no barriers between you and your greatest love?

> **They were one physically.** Genesis 2:24 says, "The two are united into one." They enjoyed sex in the way it was created. Adam was so taken with Eve when she was created he burst out, "At last! In other words, I've been waiting for the love of my life—now I am fully complete This (creation) is bone of my bone and flesh from my flesh. She will be called wo-man because she

was taken from me!" (Genesis 2:23)

They were one emotionally. They kept no secrets between each other. They fully and completely knew and accepted one another. They were best friends. They were so connected they didn't even have to finish their sentences because they knew what the other was thinking. They had a depth within their relationship we all long to experience. They truly belonged to one another!

They were one spiritually. They knew their Father, and lived in constant communion with him. They had his DNA, and were created in his image. They carried his characteristics, had his heartbeat, and knew he loved them completely and unconditionally!

They were one vocationally. They both knew their roles within the Garden, and enjoyed each and every moment creating, governing, and stewarding life in their domain.

Life was in the Garden.

Death didn't exist. Everything was created to live.

Can you imagine having plants that never stopped blooming and never died?

Prosperity was in the Garden.

Adam and Eve never had to wonder where their next rent check was coming from. They didn't have to worry about their line of credit so they could finance their business. They never skimped, penny pinched, or went without. They had absolutely everything they needed.

Safety was in the Garden.

They were never threatened by abuse or violence. They didn't have to worry about who was lurking outside their door. They could eat, sleep and work in total peace and security.

Freedom was in the Garden.

They weren't in debt to anyone. Ungrateful employers didn't oppress them. They weren't on opposite sides of a country, a tribe or a gang. They had complete freedom to shape their day, their relationships, and their work, free of obstacles. Adam and Eve were naked and felt no shame. This is the world God intended for us. We were never meant to suffer or experience shame. I think about that all the time.

Life without shame.

Can you imagine it? I think it would be heaven on earth!

Reflect:

1. *Think back*: Where in your life is there evidence of the consequences of broken connection?

2. *Take inventory:* Which of the words that describe what exists in heaven is most inviting to you? What, right now, sounds the most life-giving, most refreshing, most like a lifeline?

3. *Dream forward:* How will you move towards heavenly realities? What is one movement you could take in your daily actions, or in your thought life, to move away from shame and its brokenness?

Do Something:

Go Green! Plant something or tend something. Depending on the season and your living situation, find something living to care for. Think of God's garden. Create, or care for, one of your own. Plant a seed. Pull a weed. Buy a houseplant, water a neighbor's garden, grow a garden. Let the attention you spend tending remind you of Eden's opportunities of life, prosperity, freedom, and safety.

CHAPTER 5

THE DOWNWARD SPIRAL OF SHAME

The official definition of shame is "a painful emotion caused by a strong sense of guilt, embarrassment, unworthiness or disgrace." (freedictionary.com)

I like to define shame as "the overwhelming sense of unworthiness that overtakes everything around us." It's the feeling of wanting to run and hide and never come out. It's the sense of "What are people going to think?" It's the fear of being made fun of and humiliated.

Shame researcher Brené Brown states that shame asks two questions: Am I good enough? Who do you think you are to believe that you could... (fill in the blank)?

She distinguishes the difference between shame and guilt as shame believing "I am a mistake." and guilt believing "I *made* a mistake."

Watch the video: *Brené Brown Ted Talks on Shame.* Go to http://embed.ted.com/talks/brene_brown_listening_to_shame.html

35

or scan the QR Code (If unable to view, read script at the end of the book).

That's a huge difference.

Guilt can motivate us to step up and take responsibility for our choices.

Shame is the catalyst for a long list of destructive choices.

We find most of the destructive choices in the Garden of Eden in Genesis 3.

I remember the first time I listened to Brené Brown's Ted Talks on Shame & Vulnerability.

Watch the video *Brené Brown Ted Talks on Vulnerability*. Go to https://www.ted.com/talks/brene_brown_on_vulnerability or scan the QR Code (If unable to view, read script at the end of the book).

She spent six years researching shame, and the fruit that comes from it. When she made her list, I remember thinking, "Yes! Those are the repercussions of a life of shame, and that list of shame fruit is found in Genesis 3!"

Adam and Eve made the fateful decision to eat the fruit from the Tree of the Knowledge of Good and Evil, and unleashed shame in the Garden. The fallout was devastating.

Shame, and its destructive outcomes, have been around since the beginning of time.

Here's the astounding reality of what took place in Adam and Eve's lives.

Their love story is utterly thrilling. Genesis 2 ends with the statement, *"And the man and his wife were both naked, but they felt **no shame.**"*

In just seven short verses, **a cataclysmic shift took place.**

Here's what happened:

> "Eve saw the tree was beautiful and the fruit looked delicious, and she wanted the wisdom it would give her. So she took some of the fruit and ate it. Then she gave some to her husband, Adam, who was with her, and he ate it too. *At that moment their eyes were opened,* and they suddenly **felt shame** at their **nakedness.**" (Genesis 3:6-7a)

Wow.

Do you see how quickly it happened? The leap from "Being naked and feeling no shame" to "*Suddenly* feeling shame at their nakedness." What was once pure freedom and vulnerability, became self-protection and hiding.

Adam and Eve's decision to eat from the Tree of the Knowledge of Good and Evil was the very moment the orphan spirit entered the world. It has been robbing humanity ever since.

It all starts with shame.

Shame is the entry point into a downward spiral of relational destruction—observe the progression in Genesis 3:

> "So they sewed fig leaves to cover themselves." *Loss of Vulnerability*

> "When the cool evening breezes were blowing, the man and his wife heard the Lord God (their father) walking in the garden. So, they hid from their father among the trees. Then, their father called out to Adam, 'Where are you?'

> Adam replied, "I heard you walking in the garden, so I hid. I was afraid because I was naked." *Fear and Hiding*

> "Who told you were naked?" his father asked. "Have you eaten from the tree, whose fruit I commanded you

not to eat?"

Adam replied, "It was Eve, the woman you gave me who gave me the fruit, and I ate it." *Blame and Rejection*

Then, Eve's father asked her, "What have you done?"

"The serpent deceived me," Eve replied. "That's why I ate it." *Excuses*

After God cursed the serpent he faced his children, Adam and Eve, with their consequences.

He said to Eve,

"I will sharpen the pain of your pregnancy, and in pain you will give birth.

And you will desire to control your husband, but he will rule over you." *Physical Pain, Control and Unfulfilled Desire*

Then, he said to Adam,

"Since you listened to your wife and ate from the tree whose fruit I commanded you not to eat, the ground is cursed because of you. All your life you will struggle to scratch a living from it." *Apathy, Vocational Struggle, Hopelessness*

It's quite a list, isn't it?

Shame is the entry point to massive relational breakdown.

It opens the door to

- Loss of Vulnerability
- Fear
- Hiding
- Blame
- Rejection

- Excuses
- Physical Pain
- Control
- Unfilled Desire
- Apathy
- Vocational Struggle
- Hopelessness

Shame opened the door to twelve, count them, twelve life-stealers in the Garden of Eden. It continues to do the same to us today.

Adam and Eve, *who just moments before* had a relationship filled with intimacy, vulnerability, fulfilling partnership, freedom, and trust, had suddenly experienced a massive separation.

Suddenly, Adam refers to Eve as, *"The woman you gave me."* Talk about rejection. Can you imagine how she felt?

She didn't wait around to hold the bag, however. She quickly looked at the serpent and made him the excuse for her decision.

Now, both Adam and Eve had distanced themselves from their fabulous father and broken off their intimate relationship with each other.

Read the list again.

How many of these have you experienced?

How many do you currently experience, on a daily basis, or maybe even a moment-to-moment basis?

Here's the reality: **All life-killers originate from the orphan spirit.**

Often, **this process starts with shame.**

Reflect:

1. *Look back*: Identify some of the key moments when you experienced life stealers as a child.

2. *Take inventory*: What life stealers are you currently experiencing? Debt? Fear? Anxiety? Lack of sleep? Broken relationships? Others from the list above? Your own additions?

3. *Dream forward:* If nothing changed, how would your life look in 10 years? How much of your life would be eaten away by the consequences of shame?

Do Something:

Watch *Good Will Hunting*, and pay attention to the patterns and havoc of shame on the lives of the characters.

CHAPTER 6

JESUS IS THE ONLY SON WHO NEVER EXPERIENCED THE ORPHAN SPIRIT

I believe, deep down, we like to think of Jesus as a superhero - that way, we don't have to take his invitation seriously to do the things he did - you know, like heal blind people, stop raging storms, feed 5,000 hungry people, and resurrect his friend who was dead in a grave for several days.

The truth however, is that Jesus had a pretty regular life growing up.

He had siblings, he helped his father Joseph in the family carpenter shop, he went to church, and he journeyed to Jerusalem with his extended family for the Jewish feasts.

He had a pretty regular life, that is, until he met up with his cousin John the Baptist and became baptized. At that moment, everything shifted!

Here's what happened:

One day Jesus came from Nazareth in Galilee (his hometown), and John (the Baptist) baptized him in the

Jordan River. As Jesus came up out of the water, he saw the heavens splitting apart and the Holy Spirit descending on him like a dove. And a voice from heaven said, "You are my dearly loved son, and you bring me great joy." (Mark 1:9-11)

Some versions also include: "You bring me great pleasure. You are my beloved son with whom I am well pleased. You are my Son, chosen and marked by my love, pride of my life."

In that moment, everything came together.

Jesus heard the voice of affirmation of his Heavenly Father.

He was solidified in his identity as a beloved son who pleases his father.

He also received the power to walk in his identity when the dove, representing the Holy Spirit, descended upon him.

While I am sure Jesus wanted to bask in the glory of the moment, he didn't have that chance. Mark 1:13 tells us, *"Immediately the Spirit **drove** him into the wilderness."* The Message says, "At once, this same Spirit **pushed** Jesus out into the wild." Another version states, "Jesus was **compelled** into the wilderness."

Drove. Pushed. Compelled.

Jesus was in the desert, the dry dusty place, all alone.

- He didn't have anyone giving him kudos for his behavior.
- He didn't have food, so his body became weak.
- He didn't have the distractions of web surfing, YouTube, Facebook or Instagram to distance himself from the test.

For forty days and nights in the wilderness, he was tempted

and tested by Satan. Over and over, the Devil taunted Jesus, looking for any weakness, any area he could "own" Jesus. Can you imagine the torture?

Interestingly, the Devil's taunting continually started with the statement, "If you are the son of God..."

The Devil went after the very place where Jesus' heavenly father had just affirmed and identified him.

Satan wanted to distract and dismantle Jesus' brand new identity not just as the son of God, but as the beloved son who brings the father great joy.

Not to be thwarted, Jesus believed his father.

He took his affirmation and stepped into the full identity as a beloved son.

Because Jesus did this, he was able to resist the devil's temptations, taunts, tests, and torture for 40 full days. He not only resisted the devil, he defeated him. Luke 4:13 tells us, "the devil left him until the next opportunity."

Jesus is the only one who has ever been completely free from the orphan identity. We know this, because after 40 days of relentless testing, the Devil couldn't find any area to put his hooks into him.

We know this, because Jesus knew his father and knew he was good. He could be trusted, and he had Jesus' best interest at heart.

When we know our heavenly parent is good, completely trustworthy, and motivated to bring about our own good, we can **reclaim our true identity** as the beloved child in our heavenly family.

- Jesus could have felt abandoned by his heavenly father because his earthly father was dead.

- He could have been angry at his heavenly father because

his earthly father was poor.

- He could have been hurt, because his earthly father didn't really understand or listen to him.

But, he didn't project any of those feelings onto his heavenly father, because he had spent enough time with him to know the depths of his father's love, his total unconditional acceptance for him as his son, and his pathway to fulfilling his destiny and calling.

How about you?

- Has your earthly father had his own agenda for your life and failed to discover and encourage "who you truly are?"
- Has your earthly father failed to provide for you?
- Has your earthly father left your family? Have you lived with rejection and abandonment?
- Has your earthly father been critical and demanding, never allowing you to "feel good enough?"
- Has your earthly father failed you by... fill in the blank?

Here's our challenge.

Our adversary, the Devil, the same one who relentlessly tempted, tested and taunted Jesus, does the same to us.

He goes overboard to destroy our earthly fathers so they disappoint and fail us, just so we will project our belief system about our earthly father onto our heavenly father.

That's his scheme.

It worked with Adam and Eve, and it still works with us.

And so, our challenge begins with an intentional decision to believe the truth about both our fathers.

The truth is, our earthly father did the best he could, with his own challenges.

The even greater truth is our heavenly father moved heaven and earth to show us the depth of his love for us. He sent his first son Jesus to earth, to show us who he is. He sent his first son, Jesus, to die the most painful death imaginable, *so that you could live.*

Pay attention to this reality found in Romans 8:

> So, what do you think? With God on our side like this, how can we lose?
>
> If God didn't hesitate to put everything on the line for us, embracing our condition and exposing himself to the worst by sending his own Son, is there anything else he wouldn't gladly and freely do for us?
>
> And who would dare tangle with God by messing with one of God's chosen?
>
> Who would dare even to point a finger?
>
> The One who died for us—who was raised to life for us is in the presence of God at this very moment *sticking up for us.*
>
> Do you think anyone is going to be able to drive a wedge between us, and Christ's love for us?
>
> There is no way!
>
> Not trouble, not hard times, not hatred, not hunger, not homelessness, not bullying threats, not backstabbing, not even the worst sins listed in Scripture.
>
> None of this fazes us because Jesus loves us.
>
> I'm absolutely convinced that nothing—nothing living or dead, angelic or demonic, today or tomorrow, high or low, thinkable or unthinkable—absolutely *nothing* can get between us and God's love because of the way that Jesus our

Master has embraced us.

To be free, it is imperative that we discover who our heavenly father truly is, instead of listening to the devil's lies about his character.

Only once we discover the depth of his love for us, his motivation to bless us and bring about our best, can we then step into the fullness of our place in his family, as a beloved child in whom he has great delight and joy!

Reflect:

1. *Look back:* What qualities did you appreciate about your dad growing up? Or, if you didn't have a dad, what qualities in a grandpa, father figure, or family friend, did you most appreciate?

2. *Take inventory:* Do you think of God as Father? Is that a comforting image/metaphor? Does thinking of God as Father create a stumbling block in your pursuit of intimacy or realness in a relationship with God? What lies about God linger in your mind?

3. *Dream Forward:* Ask God to be your Dad, through simple prayers, said either once, or over and over. Think about what it would be to accept God as the loving Father who looks at you and says, "You are my beloved child, with whom I am greatly pleased."

Do Something:

Write out the words of Romans 8 verses in your journal, on sticky notes, on your bathroom mirror, or anywhere else you might see them. Read them out loud, and begin to change your mind this week.

CHAPTER 7

A PROPOSAL, SOME PIGS, AND A BIG PARTY

When God wanted to give people a picture of who he is, he chose to tell a story. This story is probably the most recognized story in the Bible. I believe the reason is because our spirits are hungry to know the true heart of our father.

So, let's imagine the scene when Jesus told it:

> His audience was diverse. It included the most religious people and the biggest rebels around. The "religious" people were offended that Jesus would even acknowledge the "rebellious" people because after all, they caused so many problems in their culture by not following all the "rules."

Watch the video: *Compassionate Father*. Go to https://vimeo.com/97771272 or scan the QR Code (If unable to view, read script at the end of the book).

Did you know the titles written before passages in the Bible are written by editors to help guide us? I don't think the editor who entitled Jesus' dramatic story knew about God's invitation to be adopted into God's family, because he, like most of us, focused on the rebellion of the younger son, rather than the astounding compassion and forgiveness shown by the father.

I like to call this story "**The Compassionate Father**" instead, because it helps me to remember all the ways he loved both his sons.

*He loved his younger son too much to seek to **control** him.*

He exercised tough love, and met his request for an early inheritance, knowing all the while he would hit bottom. In his heart, he hoped and prayed for his younger son to come home, but he didn't know for sure it would happen. This is sacrificial love; the kind that involves not knowing the outcome.

He loved his older son too much to ignore him.

When the party was in full swing, it would have been easy to forget that his older son was nowhere to be found. So, he left the party to seek him out. He found him outside seething; refusing to come in, because after all, he had followed all the "rules" and where did that get him?

In his answer, ***"All these years I've slaved for you and you never even gave me..."*** Notice he used the word "slave." He didn't understand his father's generosity, but most of all, he missed his father's heart for relationship. The father responded by calling him "My Dear Son," and stating "everything I have is yours."

This is covenant relationship in action. **Everything the father has is available to his kids.** He didn't withhold from his *rebellious* younger son and he didn't withhold from his *religious rule following* older son.

Think about your life.

- Where have you believed the lie that because you are so "rebellious," you will never get it right, and that God gave up on you a long time ago?

- Where have you believed the lie that because you have followed all the "rules religiously," you should be honored and accepted above everyone else?

Here's the part Jesus' audience didn't understand, and we seem to miss it too - even after two thousand years.

It's not our rebellion or our religious rule-following that matters.

It's our relationship with our father that changes everything.

He comes flying down the road the moment we come around the bend, never waiting for an explanation for why we don't measure up. He's too busy putting on our coat of identity, covering our dusty feet with new shoes which take us out of slavery, and unbelievably, placing the family credit card back in our hands.

He doesn't hustle us back inside, in case one of the neighbors might see us. Instead, he calls all his neighbors and friends to come and celebrate. All he really cares about in the end is that we are with him.

It's our relationship with our father that matters as well, for those of us who are busy doing all the right things.

Frankly, I don't think that he cares that much about "what we do." Instead, it's what we believe about him and ourselves that matters, because what we believe has influence in how we relate to him.

We have a heavenly father who wants a relationship with us!

You have a heavenly parent who wants to be your Dad!

He wants to show you what a faithful, forgiving, compassionate and generous father looks and acts like. He wants to teach you how to be a child in his family.

Here's the reality check for all of us.

The rebellious son came home. However, we are left wondering if the older son ever came into the party.

Could it be that those who appear or dress like a church goer, are actually farther away from the Father than those dressed in sexual ambiguity, poverty, prison clothing, or masks of losses, pain, and hurt? Perhaps pride pushes us further from God than addiction, doubt, or anger.

Reflect:

1. *Look back:* Have you lived most of your life in religious rule following or rebellion?

2. *Take inventory:* How does the statement, "Jesus is radically inclusive" sit with you? Who is it hardest for you to believe that Jesus loves and would welcome home?

3. *Dream Forward:* What is the hardest thing for you to offer up to God's unconditional, completely restorative, always forgiving Love?

Do Something:

Take a walk from your house. Go for at least 10 minutes in one direction, if possible. Stop, turn around and head back home. As you come home, imagine God, the Father, running towards you. What excuses do you have for your absence? What forgiveness are you begging for him to give? What, instead, does it feel like to just be quiet and let the consuming arms of Christ come around you, accepting you just as you are?

CHAPTER 8

WHAT'S YOUR ADDRESS?

Lots of us know about living in multiple houses. We may live with our mom during the week, and our dad on the weekends or in the summer. Some of us actually go back and forth each week, so much so that it becomes difficult to remember our true address.

If we think about this idea spiritually, we can understand the thief's desire to keep us moving in and out of his house of rebellion and religion, just so we may never get to the house of relationship.

However, the choice is really up to us.

You can decide which house you want to live within, throwing away the keys to the other houses forever.

You can choose the ***House of Rebellion***.

> Living outside the lines, making sure that no one controls you, or no rules restrain you, can make you

51

think that you are safe from rejection or judgment. The party seems great for a while, but if you are really honest with yourself, it starts to feel shallow. A perpetual party doesn't satisfy our deep longing for love, acceptance, and community.

You can choose the ***House of Religious Rule Following.***

Following the rules can make you feel safe and entitled. After all, you've done the right thing. You've worked really hard. Never absent, always on time, you've perpetually showed up. With this resume, surely you can satisfy the desire to be accepted and loved. Surely you will know you are good enough; you will be given approval.

It's exhausting to live with a long list to "need to do's" for acceptance. The Jewish people understood religious exhaustion in Jesus' day. They had over 400 rules to follow for one day of the week: their Sabbath day of rest. 400 plus rules?! That doesn't sound restful to me, does it to you? They were drowning in all the rules; and the rules didn't draw them closer to their Heavenly Father. They also believed just one misstep would send them outside the *House of Religion*—so the pressure was ever-intensifying.

For us, there's good news.

We can permanently leave both the ***House of Rebellion*** and the ***House of Religious Rule Following,*** and move into the ***House of Relationship.***

The movers are all ready to clean out the two Houses. They are sorting all that shouldn't come with us to the *House of Relationship:* the orphan identity and all its destructive fruit of fear, hiding, addiction, insecurity, unworthiness, isolation, past pain, regrets, un-forgiveness, and the need to measure up to become worthy of love.

The ***House of Relationship*** is so different.

> Our Father runs to the door to welcome us. He throws open his arms with a big hug and begins to invite us to sit down to have a cup of tea, so he can listen to everything we say. He points out all the interesting parts of our personalities and our unique gifts, and celebrates all the ways we please him.
>
> He invites us to the dinner table. He calls out for us to come, and pulls out our chair for us. He invites his other kids to hear about our day, encouraging us to listen to their stories.
>
> He calls us into the Great Room to play—to be kids again, silly and fun, laughing from the depths of our bellies. He encourages us to create. After all, we were created to create.
>
> He tucks us into bed. He is careful to make sure we are safe and comfortable. He prays with us, telling us one last time just how beloved we are, and how valuable we are to him. He hugs us, and smiles as he leaves the room.

Does this sound too good to be true?

If so, you have been the victim of a great theft.

Jesus told us a great truthful reality in John 10:10, when he said,

> "The thief has come to steal, kill and destroy. But, I have come to give you a rich and fulfilling life."

Here's my reality.

The more I've agreed with my father's goodness and his desire to share his good gifts with me, the more I have been able to experience them. Sometimes, they are so over-the-top they leave me breathless.

Here is one example.

> It started with a desire. A friend of mine described her experience of vacationing in Tuscany, Italy. I began to dream about what it would be like to go to the same Tuscan Villa she visited, as it sounded heavenly. I had not told anyone about my desire.
>
> Suddenly, our three grown children came up with the idea for us to go to Italy as a family. The first reservation we made? The villa in Tuscany.
>
> I had been dreaming of the moment of arriving at the Villa for months, as my friend had described a great big welcome basket that would greet us.
>
> I had also created a wedding book for our daughter, who was married the previous year, and was looking forward to giving it to her and her husband when we got to the Villa.
>
> We toasted to our arrival in Tuscany and explored all the rooms and grounds. Afterwards, I gave Luke and Heather their book. As they pored over it, I sat there, thinking, "Wow, Father, you are fulfilling my heart's desire. Can it get any better than this?"
>
> But God's good gifts didn't stop there. It began to rain, just for a few minutes, but right as they finished absorbing their book, the rain stopped and a giant double rainbow appeared outside. Amazingly, as we ran outside to experience it I realized we could see both the beginning and ending of the rainbow, as well as all seven colors!
>
> The joy we felt at that moment overflowed. It truly felt like heaven coming to earth!

That night, I couldn't sleep. As I played solitaire on my iPad, I suddenly had a sense of my father wanting to tell me something.

Here's what I wrote in my journal:

> "I was playing solitaire and I sensed you being like a Dad who hid Christmas presents under the tree and couldn't wait to delight his kids-to please them, to sacrifice so they could have the best Christmas ever.

> I envisioned you jumping up and down saying, 'Did you see what I did for you, Tamara?' I gave you that rainbow as a sign of my pleasure for you."

I wrote down a Scripture that night which may be helpful to you:

> "You parents, if your children ask for a loaf of bread, do you give them a stone? Or if they ask for a fish, do you give them a snake? Of course not! If sinful people give good gifts to their children, how much more will your heavenly father give GOOD GIFTS to those who ask him." Matthew 7:9-11

The context of this Scripture is important. I believe the Sermon on the Mount, Matthew 5-7, encompasses Jesus' core teachings, the ones he taught over and over everywhere that he traveled.

And since Jesus, who was God's first son, thought it was important, so should we.

This is the second part of my journaling from that night:

> "I started to think about how I would like to blog this one day, and I started to realize that many might interpret it as bragging. I think there's often a pressure to keep our reception of God's good gifts to ourselves because it might make others feel bad.

> But, I sense you wanting me to acknowledge the gift; you want me to see you as the kind of dad who likes to give his

kids good gifts.

It's not that you love me more than everyone else; it's what I have chosen to agree with."

I've agreed that:

- You are a good dad who loves his kids
- You are a good dad who created a safe and loving place for us to live in the Garden
- You are a dad who wants us to enjoy the good gifts you have given us
- You are a dad who wants us to prosper

If you are one who experienced a twinge of jealousy or sadness or even anger at my story, then it's a clue for you to consider recognizing the fact the orphan identity has already stolen a great deal from you.

It's time for you to pack up your bags and to leave your *Houses of Rebellion* and *Religious Rule Following*. Prepare to move instead to the *House of Relationship* with your heavenly father, who absolutely adores you and who wants to bring his good gifts into your life.

Reflect:

1. *Look back:* What different houses have you lived in in your life? What was characteristic of the mood and energy inside each place?

2. *Take Inventory:* What most directs your living space right now? Do you use your house as a place of rest? A place to work? A place to be alone? A place to enjoy friendship and community?

3. *Dream Forward:* What would it look like to accept Jesus' radically inclusive, completely free, wonderfully

loving invitation to move into a relationship with him?

Do Something:

Look at the affirmations about a good dad a few paragraphs back. Which is hardest to believe? Put them up, in your own handwriting, in your current house. Read them. Speak them. Let them sink down into your head and heart.

CHAPTER 9

MOVING HOUSES

A few years ago, my husband Bill and I moved from Seattle to Santa Rosa, CA. Our goal was to be in California by New Year's Day. Two days after Christmas, the movers arrived. I had awakened early in order to be with my heavenly father as I sought his comfort for the big transition ahead of us, when suddenly I heard a HUGE noise. When I looked outside, a giant moving truck was coming down the street. Behind it followed several other cars. As I continued to watch, people in moving uniforms came out of the cars and walked toward our front door.

Within minutes of their arrival, our house was filled with packers in almost every room. They were so thorough that after two days, the entire contents of our house was ready to be loaded into the van. My role in the move was to ensure that everything that was meant to go to our new home found its way into the moving van, and everything that we wanted to leave behind was placed in a pile in the garage for donation.

Your role in the move from the *Houses of Rebellion and Religion* is to acknowledge what should be left in those houses, (not passed onto others!), and *to identify what you want to move* **into** *the House of Relationship.*

Your heavenly father wants to give you spiritual currency to go shopping for those items you might not yet possess for your new house.

Do Something:

Here's a process you can use to clean out and pack. You may want to invite a friend to do this with you, or to do it with a group:

Take a piece of paper, your tablet, (or use a white board, if with a group) and make two columns:

ORPHAN IDENTITY	ADOPTED IDENTITY
Orphan Identity	Adopted Daughter/Son Identity
Fear	Security
Anger	Peace
Rejected	Chosen
Scarcity	Abundance

Under the two columns, identify the areas that belong to adoption and to orphan. Pay particular attention to the areas you identify within the orphan spirit. It is helpful to think of the opposites. For example: fear (orphan), security (adoption), or anger (orphan), peace (adoption). This is also important for the process below.

> When you believe your list is complete, state this prayer out loud:

> Heavenly Father, thank you for being my Daddy, my Papa, my Abba. I am glad that I have been adopted into your family. I am tired of living like an orphan. I want to be set free from the orphan identity. Thank you for sending your Son Jesus to redeem me from the slavery that leads me into fear, and to bring me into the place of adoption as your child.

> I confess I have lived as an orphan, and I bind its presence in my life now.

> I confess the fruit of the orphan identity, (name one of the words you wrote on the orphan column), and lock it now. Instead, I replace it with (the opposite spirit on the adoption column).

(Continue this process until you have gone through the entire list.)

Now that I have confessed all the fruits of the orphan identity, I take the orphan identity, and I completely forbid it from ever operating in my life again. I joyfully replace it with the adoption identity as your beloved (son) or (daughter).

> I thank you heavenly Father, that my identity is as your beloved child, and I am knitted into your heart. I am part of your family, and I live in your house. Thank you that you are teaching me how to live in your house in my role as your child. Amen.

Journal about your experience, and if possible, share your process with the important people in your life. Take time daily to declare who you are as God's beloved child, upon whom He lavishes his love! (The more you speak it out, the sooner you will learn how to live in the Father's *House of Relationship!*)

CHAPTER 10

REMOVING STUCK PLACES

N ow that you've vacated the *House of Rebellion* and the *House of Religious Rule Following* and moved into the *House of Relationship*, it's time to decorate your new house.

Perhaps you remember a packing process. For a friend, the summer before she began college was filled with anticipation and preparation. She had a list of what you would need for school (extra-long twin sheets, a shower curtain), along with some suggestions (lamps, clocks, decorations). There were four possible sizes of rooms in her assigned dorm, and there was no way to know for sure what would fit. She packed as much as possible in her car and drove to the dorm, her car as stuffed as the teddy bear plastered in the back window. When she saw how dismally small her room was and that her roommate had already claimed more than half the space, she had to remove the extras and keep essentials. Like a funnel, the big mess of stuff became streamlined into what would make the most of her freshman year.

You may feel the same way.

You may wonder, "What will my new house look like?"

You may wonder what your heavenly father may want you to buy with your heavenly currency. This is normal as we transition from one mindset, or home, to another.

To help you work through these questions, I developed a process that I call, the **Funnel Exercise.**

A funnel is a helpful tool in a kitchen, science lab, garage, even a child's bathtub. A funnel gathers something large and dispersed, delivering it directly to a focused destination and avoiding spillovers.

Here's the deal: Earlier, we explored the fact that Jesus is the only person who has ever lived on earth without being affected by the orphan identity. There is a reason for this. Jesus doesn't have any clogs in his funnel.

Let me explain. When Jesus was baptized, Mark tells us, "the heavens ripped open," (Mark 1:9) and the dove landed on him. I like to think about the heavens coming to earth in a funnel, because this helps me to make sense of Jesus' call to do "the things I do and even greater things than this?" (John 14:12-14)

One day, I suddenly "got" it.

Jesus has no clogs in his funnel.

Nothing keeps God's love and power flowing freeing from heaven into him, so it can flow out of him to others.

So basically, Jesus was able to make the miracles he did, because the power of heaven was continually pouring out and he was consistently able to receive the resources of heaven to demonstrate the Kingdom of God.

We, however, do have clogs in our own funnels.

Just like the clogs in our toilets that may keep them from flushing, our clogs prevent us from being a completely clear conduit of God's love and power.

The day I had my initial experience of discovering the reality of the adoption spirit, God gave me a clear picture of my own funnel. It was bent in the middle so not much could get past the bend. Once he straightened it out I felt a rush of love, beyond what I ever imagined could be possible.

Romans 5:5:

> "And hope does not put us to shame, because God's love has been poured out into our hearts through the Holy Spirit, who has been given to us."

In Greek, the original language, this verse reads more exactly, *"God's love continually pours into our hearts."* When God's love bucket tips, it isn't a one-time pouring. Instead, this is love flowing to us non-stop, over and over, always and anywhere.

I experienced the pouring out of God's love for three days, and then the experience suddenly stopped. I was really bummed, so I asked my father what was going on.

He shared with me, "I didn't stop my flow of love. I just removed the physical experience of it so that you would live with the reality of where so many of my children live, so your heart would be broken for them. I want you to share the depth of my non-stop flow of love, with them."

And so, I am doing that now.

God's word to us in Romans 5:5 is true. He continually pours his love into our hearts, moment by moment. The flow never ceases. The only problem is that most of our funnels from heaven to earth are clogged with spiritual debris, keeping us from experientially knowing it.

The funnel from heaven doesn't just release God's love, it also releases power.

God's word of identity affirmation represented his love, but the dove landing on Jesus represented heavenly power, which is sealed inside of us.

Ephesians 1:13 tells us:

> "And you also were included in Christ when you heard the message of truth, the gospel of your salvation. When you believed, you were **marked in him with a seal,** the promised Holy Spirit."

Jesus lived on earth filled with his father's love and the Holy Spirit's power. We must realize, Jesus had **the same amount** of his father's love poured continually into him **as we have**. He had the same power of the Holy Spirit as a human, as we are given. Jesus, however, didn't have any clogs in his funnel!

Do Something:

Our next opportunity is to identify our Funnel-Cloggers, and to plunge them right out!

Here's the process:

1. Pray before you begin this process, and ask your heavenly father to show you the clogs he wants to plunge.

2. You will need a bowl, some small sheets of paper, a toilet paper roll or another funnel which can be plunged of the papers, and some salt

3. The salt represents God's love and power flowing from heaven.

4. Before you start to identify your funnel-stuffers, pour the salt into the funnel. Watch how it flows unhindered

without any clogs. Think about Jesus' certainty about his identity as his father's beloved son, with whom he is extremely delighted!

This is a list of some clogs (and explanations) that may be in your funnel. It isn't an exhaustive list, but it can get you started:

1. *Identity Challenges:* areas of our identity formed by our parents, or others, that go against Scripture, worldly messages, or our own definition.

2. *Un-forgiveness:* refusal to let others (including God and ourselves) off the hook for sins they have committed against us, either purposefully or unintentionally.

3. *Trust Issues with God:* Areas where broken trust brings the question "Is God for me? Does he have my best at heart?"

4. *Ungodly beliefs:* Belief systems (usually formed early in life) that contradict Scripture (for example: I am not worthy... to be protected, heard, respected).

5. *Agreements with the enemy:* Areas where we have aligned with truths that contradict Scripture (for example: I am... dumb, clumsy, ugly).

6. *Defense Mechanisms:* Decisions and actions we commit when we are stressed, hurt, ashamed, or suffering (for example: isolation, addiction, anger).

7. *Ungodly Soul Ties:* Relationships in our past or present that are destructive or take us away from God's purposes in our lives (all sexual relationships outside of the covenant of marriage are ungodly soul ties).

8. *Generational sins and curses:* Family traits passed

knowingly or unknowingly to ourselves, with negative impact on our lives (for example: known events like divorce or suicide, or often unknown events, like agreements our ancestors made with the enemy which continue to affect us).

9. *Behavioral sin:* Actions we take outside of God's boundaries for us. Why do you think behavioral sin is the last item on this list?

Our beliefs determine our actions.

What we tell ourselves about who God is, and who we are, defines our choices. Our outward behaviors are only the symptoms of what we hold and carry within our heart and heads

When we understand our true identity and hold the belief system that God is a good father who wants to bless his children (read blog at http://tamarabuchan.com/2014/11/mrs-doubtfire-the-sacrificial-father), we begin to make good choices that fulfill our lives, rather than continually open the door to the one who steals life and love from us.

As you identify your own funnel-cloggers, write each one on a piece of the small paper. Stuff the paper pieces into your funnel. Take your time during this process. You have many years of clogs - the first plunge can feel rather daunting, but it is SO WORTH IT!

As you consider your clogs, keep in mind this truth:

> "No matter what situation your life is in right now, no matter what your past is, no matter your despair about the future, you are completely loved and completely empowered right now. The only thing stopping the experiential flow of God's love and power is your funnel clogs."

After you identify your funnel clogs, go to the bowl with

the salt alongside it. Use an empty toilet paper holder to signify Jesus' funnel, and watch the salt (representing God's love and Spirit power) flow freely. Consider what his experience of freedom must have felt like.

Now, pour salt through your own funnel. Does anything come out?

Take a funnel plunger (anything will do) to represent Jesus' forgiveness. Plunge out all your clogs, as you thank Jesus for his gift of freedom in your life. Pour the salt again through the empty funnel, and celebrate the level of freedom you are now experiencing. Jesus came to eradicate your funnel clogs. His willingness to exchange his life for yours showed the depth of his love for you. When he intentionally gave his body to be beaten, his spirit to be shamed and humiliated, and his life to be crucified, the blood that flowed from his body, set you free.

Here is your reality:

You have new furnishings for your new home! *The House of Relationship* is filled with gifts of comfort, beauty, and belonging. Recognize your possessions from the *House of Rebellion* and *House of Religious Rule Following*, which are locked up, never to be retrieved again!

Reflect:

1. *Look back*: Was there repetition or a theme in your funnel clogs? What category took up the most space?

2. *Take inventory:* What reflections do you have about the funnel exercise? What insights did you gain? What questions do you still have?

3. *Dream forward:* Imagine a daily funnel clearing and the freedom this will bring you. Make a commitment to partner with Jesus for a daily plunge!

CHAPTER 11

SIGNING THE ADOPTION CERTIFICATE

Wow. Look how far you've come! Let's pause and look back.

Reflect.

Look back. We've read about ancient Roman adult adoptions, a tiny, terrified orphan girl too shaken to accept new love, a compassionate Father who embraces both his sons, and the process of moving, which involves a cleaning out, packing up, and location change. What is different in your heart and head now?

Take inventory. What remains unsettled? Did any of the stories not "work" for you? What questions do you have that are yet unanswered?

Dream forward: Do the work of figuring out what lingers

vaguely. Revisit that section of the book, read the scriptures around the quoted text for greater context. Email us with your questions. We would love to help you embrace these truths, to step into your new identity, and to move into the house of relationship. (tamarabuchan@gmail.com or lindseyosborne@gmail.com)

Do Something:

Let's celebrate your adoption and your unique place within God's family. Do you remember the description of Roman adoptions in the first century when Paul wrote about the adoption in Romans 8?

Looking at the adult to be adopted, a Roman judge would say, "_____, your past is now completely wiped clean. Everything that came before is now erased. You have a fresh start, you have support from the mentors who will train you in how to live within your new family, and you have parents who love you and want you in their home."

With great fanfare, the judge would take his rag and wipe the parchment clean. He would then write the adoptee's new name on the parchment, along with places for the new parents and seven mentors to sign.

Today, the judge is speaking to you.

Your place in God's family is both secure and permanent. The ink is indelible and can never be erased. Just like the ancient adoptees, you will have a new name with your adoption:

Read Ephesians 3:14-21:

> For this reason I kneel before the Father, from *whom every family in heaven and on earth derives its name.*
>
> I pray that out of his glorious riches, he may strengthen you with power through his Spirit in your inner being, so that Christ may dwell in your hearts through faith.

And I pray that you, being rooted and established in love, may have the power, together with all the Lord's holy people, to grasp how wide and long and high and deep is the love of Christ, and to know the love that surpasses knowledge—that you may be filled to the measure of all the fullness of God.

Now to him who is able to do immeasurably more than all we ask or imagine, according to his power that is at work within us, to him be glory in the church and in Christ Jesus throughout all generations, for ever and ever! Amen.

We walk out the orphan to adoption process, the funnel plunging and signing adoption certificates at the Reclaim Identity Retreat.

Watch the video: *Reclaim Identity Retreat.* Go to http://vimeo.com/95551009 or scan the QR Code (If unable to watch the video, read script at the end of the book).

I am always amazed at how clever God is, in giving people new names. However, many don't receive their names right away. They come later at a special time that their Heavenly Father has prepared.

Take some time now to pray and to ask God whether he wants to give you your new name now, or to wait until later. It will come! If you have an idea after your prayer, that is your name! If you don't understand it, ask the Lord what it means. Don't try to over-analyze it. Accept it and own it!

Sometimes, your given name is your new name. My parents named me Tamara Jean, but they always called me Tammy growing up. Something within me always made me feel that being called Tammy wasn't right.

When we were about to make our first big move from

Denver to Seattle, I received some ministry and the first statement they gave me was "God is giving you a new name."

I thought to myself, "That settles it. I am going to go by Tamara now." It took some time, but now even my family calls me Tamara. Every time I hear it, I know this is the name God gave me. What does it mean? I tell the story in *Identity Crisis: Reclaim the True You* of how God confirmed for me how important my name is to him and his purposes for my life.

Signing your Adoption Certificate:.

Print Adoption Certificate at http://www.ReclaimIdentity.org.

Imagine the Judge before you speaking these words: (Speak them out loud)

> "_____, your past is now completely wiped clean. Everything that came before is now erased. You have a fresh start, you have support from your mentors, and you have parents who love you and want you to be part of their family."

Now read Ephesians 3:14-21 out loud (it is personalized for you):

> "For this reason I kneel before the Father, from whom every family in heaven and on earth derives its name.
>
> I pray that out of his glorious riches he may strengthen me with power through his Spirit in my inner being, so that Christ may dwell in my heart through faith. And I pray that I, being rooted and established in love, may have power, together with all the Lord's family, to grasp how wide and long and high and deep is the love of Christ, 19 and to know this love that surpasses knowledge—that I may be filled to the measure of all the fullness of God.
>
> Now to him who is able to do immeasurably more than

all I ask or imagine, according to his power that is at work within me, to him be glory in the church and in Christ Jesus throughout all generations, for ever and ever! Amen."

Now, take your certificate and sign it. Imagine your heavenly parents being present, along with your mentors. Leave your new name blank if you have not yet received it.

Because you are a valued member of God's family, consider whom those may be who would stand in as mentors. Go to them and share your process. Invite them to sign your adoption certificate. It may lead you into a greater relationship with them.

Consider finishing your process with communion, as a celebration of your status as God's adopted child!

Do Something:

Get some champagne, sparkling cider or flavored water. Buy some snacks. Toast to your new identity. Give (seven!) friends the invitation to cheer you on, to toast in affirmation of this transformation in your life. Take pictures. Write a journal entry about it. Truly celebrate your journey, your healing and your new life.

Conclusion:

Celebrate how far you've come. You are no longer living as a fearful orphan. You are secure in your father's family. You have all your resources available to him.

You are known.

You are valued.

You are seen.

You are heard.

You are loved.

Now is the time to take all that you have learned and implement it. It takes a new brain path 90 days to full complete the process. *Our Marvelous Minds* blog at http://tamarabuchan. com/2014/11/our-marvelous-minds/. You have already spent years reinforcing your old messages. It will take some time for your brain to assimilate an opposite message.

Did you know our brain actually kicks out thoughts that don't line up with its current thinking? That's why it is vital to invest in yourself and in your future by changing your mind about your heavenly dad, your identity as his child, and the reality of your life on earth!

It's also important to state your new messages out loud. Romans 10:10 tells us:

> For it is by believing in your heart that you are made right with God, and it is by *speaking* with your mouth that you are saved."

A bit later in the same passage Paul writes, "Faith comes from hearing."

When we speak truth out loud, especially Scripture, our ears hear it and send it to our brains. When our brains hear it, they wake up and begin to align. At the same time, however, they are dismantling the old messages.

Think of it this way. A highway may be in existence for generations. This highway can be well-worn from everyone who travels upon it, sometimes to the point where the road is unable to be used as a path to one's destination. Its potholes may cause accidents, its exits can become clogged up, and excessive traffic jams may delay travel for hours.

It is readily apparent that a new highway needs to be built. So, the city begins work on the new road, but it takes time until it is ready to be used. In the meantime, cars are allowed on the parts that are ready, but still travel on the old, broken down highway.

Finally, the new highway is completed and ready to become the new artery through the city. Cement blockades are placed in front of the entryways to the old highway, and it is dismantled.

Your brain will block its own old pathways from being traveled upon any longer, but only once you've completed the new highways of truth. These new roads will take you into the places of your dreams and your destinies.

It's worth going after. You are worthy of your investment. Your heavenly father is ready to put the construction crew into action as soon as you take your step!

Watch the video: *Where Do We Go from Here?* Go to http://vimeo.com/95551868 or scan the QR Code (If unable to watch the video, read script at the end of the book).

Affirmation cards can either be online or written on index cards. (Quizlet is a helpful app http://quizlet.com/help)

SAMPLE WITH SCRIPTURE:

Lies I have believed:

- I am not good enough to be accepted.

- I will always be on the outside looking in.

- I disappoint God and other people.

Truth:

"All praise to God, the Father of our Lord Jesus Christ, who has blessed me with every spiritual blessing in the heavenly realms because I am united with Christ. Even before he made the world, God loved me and chose me in Christ to be holy and without fault in his eyes. God decided in advance to adopt me into his own family by bringing me to himself through Jesus Christ. This is what he wanted to do, and it gave him great pleasure." Ephesians 1:3-5

SAMPLE WITHOUT SCRIPTURE:

Lie I have believed:

- I am not good enough.

Truth:

- I am made in God's image. He calls me his masterpiece. I am more than good enough, I am fully accepted, fully loved and fully known.

Tamara J. Buchan is founder of Reclaim Ministries, ordained Evangelical Covenant pastor, Master of Divinity from Denver Seminary, speaker and author. However, these worldly credentials do not fulfill or thrill her nearly as much as her identity as beloved child and royal heir to her Heavenly Father. Tamara is passionate about her marriage to Bill, their adult daughters: Heather, Bonnie and Molly, and son-in-law Luke. Tamara and Bill reside in Sonoma County, California. Contact Tamara at tamarabuchan@gmail.com or visit www.ReclaimIdentity.org for information about "Reclaim Identity Retreats" in Sonoma County and availability to speak at your church or organization.

Lindsey D. Osborne is a freelance writer with a Masters of Divinity from Central Baptist Theological Seminary. She works as a Regional Trainer for Young Life and as a coach at a Crossfit affiliate. She and her husband and their three children live in Kansas City with family, grace, and adventure as hallmarks of their days and ways.

Identity Crisis: Reclaim the True You

 **What does a dried dandelion have to do with an identity crisis?** Everything, if we stop looking at it from a gardener's perspective and start to understand its hidden value. The identities we adopt from the world are like dandelions the gardener fervently attacks before they dry up into the perfect ball of seeds, which spread all over the yard when the wind begins to blow. If we think about our enemy, the Devil, as the gardener, we begin to understand his motive is to convince us that our identities are worthless weeds: throwaways when compared to the beautiful rose bushes right next to us. Our enemy, the gardener, thrives when we agree that our identities are discarded weeds, rather than boldly reclaiming our true identities from our Master Gardener: the Creator of the Universe. To reclaim is to take that which is worthless and make it beautiful and productive again. An overgrown garden with dried dandelions can appear to be worthless. However, when the Master Gardener begins to blow the seeds, our lives suddenly "wake up" and start to take root in gardens we never dreamed we could inhabit.

Available in paperback book and eBook

Spun Out on Shame? Reclaim Your Sanity

Shame literally spins us around as isolation, hopelessness, and self-condemnation, become our constant companions. God breaks into the cycle, taking our shame and spinning it into his forgiveness. As we are cleansed and set free, our lives become fresh and fully alive. *Spun out on shame? Reclaim Your Sanity*, will take your through a journey of exchanging shame for freedom... the life you were meant to experience...You were Meant for More!

Available in paperback book and eBook

Seeking The Christmas Lamb

Is your Christmas more "Santa" than "Savior"? For many, the Christmas season has become synonymous with long lines at the department store and shiny wrapping paper. And in addition to presents under the tree and eggnog, there's something about a Savior born in a manger, right? *Seeking the Christmas Lamb* is a tool for the family who wishes to slow down and find the real reason to celebrate the holidays. Borrowing from her own quest for a meaningful celebration of Advent, author Tamara J. Buchan creates a journey through the twenty-eight days leading to Christmas and the twelve days of Epiphany. Rich but simple daily readings trace God's plan for humanity, from Genesis to Revelation, pivoting on the sacrificial Advent of His Son. Through these pages, you and your family can passionately pursue an intimate understanding of the season's significance. Discover how the Christmas season can help you find a new appreciation for Christ's Advent in your own life!

Available in eBook

My Invitation

I entered into my room one morning, and sensed something was different. I came there to meet God, but I did not expect to hear the two questions that I sensed him asking me: "Do you know how much I love you? Do you know what it means to be adopted into my family?

I replied, "I guess not. Otherwise, I don't think you'd be asking me the question."

This encounter was the beginning of a wonderful, wild adventure of discovering my own "true you" - the identity my Creator had created for me, the me I am meant to be, rather than all the other identities the world gives me.

Think about it. We have identities given to us by our parents, our employers, our friends, the media and culture. We filter all these voices, and contribute our own self talk, perhaps the loudest voice of all, creating an identity light years away from the astounding identity God gives to us.

I invite you to discover for yourself the answer to God's questions, "Do you know how much I love you? Do you know what it means that I have adopted you into my family?"

Welcome to the identity journey!

Story of the Adopted Girl

I have some friends who were unable to have children. They finally gave up and pursued adoption. When they were able to adopt a 7-year-old little girl from an orphanage, they went to work preparing their house to welcome their beloved new daughter into their home and family!

The expectant parents decorated a beautiful bedroom with fluffy pink covers, a beautiful window seat filled with stuffed animals, a closet containing cute clothes, and a bathroom filled with all the lotions and potions necessary to delight a little girl.

They made a cupboard for this little girl in their kitchen in order to hold her snacks, and filled their family room with games and movies. All the while they prepared their house, they dreamed of the wonderful times they would experience sharing their day at the dinner table, playing together in the family room and tucking her into bed in her comfortable bed.

The day they went to pick her up, she came out clutching a bag of rags. They told her she wouldn't need those ragged clothes any longer, as she had brand-new clothes hanging in her closet, but she insisted on bringing them with her.

That night, they cried with joy as they tucked her into bed and said their prayers. In the middle of the night, the mother woke up unable to wait until morning to see her new child, so she tiptoed into the child's room and to her dismay, discovered that she was missing.

She frantically went to wake her husband. They searched the entire house. Finally, when they couldn't find her anywhere they looked at one another and asked, "Do you think she could be in our basement?"

The basement was an old cellar, with crickety and uneven stairs. They carefully found their way to the bottom and saw her in its corner, sleeping on concrete, clutching her bag of rags.

They woke up the little girl and said, "You don't need to sleep here, you have a beautiful bedroom upstairs." They put her back bed and went to sleep.

The next morning, their new daughter came downstairs

wearing one of her old dresses from the orphanage. They reminded her she had a closet of new clothes, but she insisted in wearing her ragged dress to school.

That night, she refused to come to the dinner table or to come into the family room to spend time with them.

Night after night, they found their beloved daughter sleeping on concrete, clutching her bag of rags.

Finally, they cried out in despair, "We've done everything and we can't seem to help you understand you are part of our family. We have planned for you, prepared a place for you in our home and our hearts. We love you and will always love you. Your past is in the past. You are wanted, accepted, cherished and secure. We will never stop trying to convince you just how much we love you. Let go of the rags and grab ahold of the treasure you deeply deserve."

Do you recognize this little girl? Could she be you? Are you holding onto the rags of your past? Is the root of your identity, so firmly entrenched that multiple invitations to move on have not set you free? What do you need to hear to move out of the basement and into the warmth of a bedroom built for you?

What do you need in order to move out of the basement and into your heavenly family?

 ## Compassionate Father

One of the reasons Jesus came to earth was to show us who his heavenly father is. He told this story to give us a picture of him. We commonly know this story as the Prodigal Son, but Jesus did not tell it to highlight the failure and shame of the prodigal, but instead to demonstrate his father's forgiveness, compassion and generosity.

There once was a father who had two sons. The older son was all about doing the right things and following the rules.

We might say that he was religious in his rule-following. The younger son was restless, bored, and rebellious. He couldn't wait to leave his father's farm.

One day, the restless son went to his father and asked for his inheritance early, so he could go explore the world. His father loved him too much to try to control him, so he gave him the money and sent him on his way with a sinking heart, wondering if he would ever see him again.

At first, the younger son had a great time. He threw party after party, and countless guests came - that is, as long as he bought the drinks. Once the money ran out however, he wasn't quite as popular. When he found himself doing the lowest thing possible - feeding the pigs, wishing he could eat their food - he came to his senses and said to himself, "In my father's house, even the servants have a house to live in and food to eat. I am not worthy to be called a son any longer, but perhaps my father will let me be a slave in his household."

So, he began the long journey home, each step getting harder as he neared home. He continued practicing his speech over and over, "Father, I am not worthy....

What he didn't know was that his father stood on his porch day after day, night after night, hoping and praying his son would come home. The day he saw his son round the bend, he took off running toward the slumped, sagging shoulders of the sauntering boy. He flew into his son, enveloping him in his arms, crying out, "My son, you were lost and now you are found. You were dead but now you are alive."

His son started his speech, "father, I am not worthy." His father cut him off and threw his coat over him. His coat was his family identity. He took shoes and put them on his bare feet, because you see slaves didn't wear shoes, and his father wanted to restore the young man's status to that of his son. And amazingly, his father gave him back the family credit card, by putting the ring on his finger...this is how they did business.

His father didn't shame him, or quickly bring him into the house to hide him from the neighbors. No - he called for the biggest party ever, to celebrate that his lost son was found, his dead son was alive.

When the older son came home, the party was in full swing. He asked one of the servants what it was for. When he heard his brother was home, He stood outside seething. He was furious that after all his work to do the right things, to follow all the rules, and to work hard, here was his brother being celebrated for rebellious behavior.

His father, with his focus on relationship, realizing his older son should be home by then, went to look for him. He found him outside, still fuming. He went to him and said, "My son, come into the party." He answered, "I can't believe this. I have slaved for you all these years and you've never thrown me a party. Now this son of yours comes home and you throw him a party. How does he deserve this?"

The Father answered, "My beloved son, everything I have is yours. It always has been. But, your brother was lost and now he is found, he was dead, but now he is alive."

The Father's desire was for a full family life for each of his sons. Regardless of past mistakes or current confusion, throwing all score sheets into the fire, the father accepts, pursues, and hosts perfect relationship with his sons...or something...about how the Father extends the invitation relentlessly.

Where Do We Go From Here?

We've had quite the journey, discovering how we have suffered identity theft and, unwittingly lived as an orphan rather than as a beloved child in our heavenly family! Now that we've reached the end of this journey, you are just now embarking on a new adventure of discovering how to re-orient yourself into life within God's family. We must let God's invitation truly transform how we live our daily lives. Our heads, hearts, and habits must be re-oriented around the reality of identity as a Child in God's family.

So, how do you take steps to make this new identity real? What support will you need for your new life?

We've developed some tools for you to use to undergird your new life as a beloved family member:

1. Continue to change your mind, using the affirmation statements you have developed. Remember: it takes 90 days to build a new brain path to fully adopt your adoption!

2. Engage other identity e-books—a great next step is "Discover Your True Purpose."

3. Go to www.ReclaimIdentity.org to listen to the podcasts: 15 Minute to focus.

APPENDIX: VIDEO SCRIPTS

CHAPTER 1
Invitation to the Identity Journey
http://vimeo.com/95551691

CHAPTER 2
Story of the Adopted Girl
https://vimeo.com/97771271

CHAPTER 5
Brené Brown Ted Talks
https://www.ted.com/talks/
brene_brown_on_vulnerability

Brené Brown Ted Talks
http://embed.ted.com/talks/brene_brown_liste-
ning_to_shame.html

CHAPTER 7
Compassionate Father
https://vimeo.com/97771272

CHAPTER 11
Reclaim Identity Retreat
http://vimeo.com/95551009

Where Do We Go From Here
http://vimeo.com/95551868